THE USBORNE
BIG BOOK OF BIG
DINOSAURS

Written by Alex Frith

Illustrated by Fabiano Fiorin

Designed by Stephen Wright
Dinosaur expert: Dr. Darren Naish

Meet the dinosaurs

Long, long ago, before there were any people, there were animals known as dinosaurs all over the world. Some of them were very, VERY big.

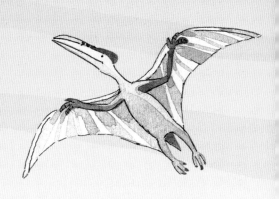

Dinosaurs were the BIGGEST animals that have ever walked on land.

Up in the sky, dinosaurs were watched by flying creatures known as pterosaurs.

No one knows exactly how big the biggest dinosaur was. But it was at least as LONG as a swimming pool, as TALL as three buses, and HEAVIER than twenty elephants.

Dinosaur babies hatched from eggs. They started out no bigger than a chick, but very soon they grew AND GREW AND GREW...

The very biggest dinosaurs

Dinosaurs came in all shapes and sizes. Some were only little, but others were absolutely ENORMOUS.

Lift the pages and see if you can spot all these dinosaurs in the scene underneath.

Compsognathus
0.7m (28 inches) long

Eoraptor
1m (3 feet) long

The VERY biggest dinosaurs are known as sauropods. They had long necks and tails, and ate plants.

Iguanodon
9m (30 feet) long

Parasaurolophus
10m (33 feet) long

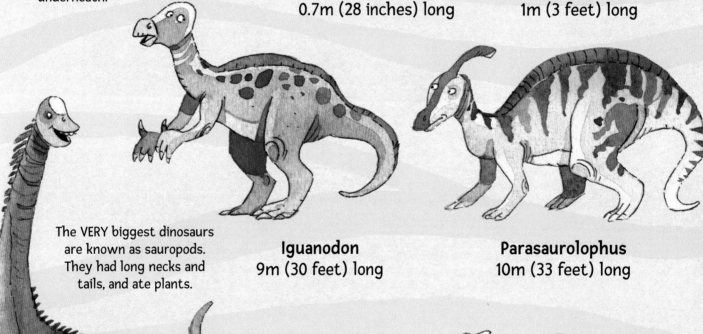

Brachiosaurus
22m (72 feet) long
Brachiosaurus could lift its head as high as six double-decker buses.

Argentinosaurus
35m (115 feet) long
Argentinosaurus probably weighed 88 tonnes (97 tons) – that's more than 10 elephants.

Apatosaurus
23m (76 feet) long

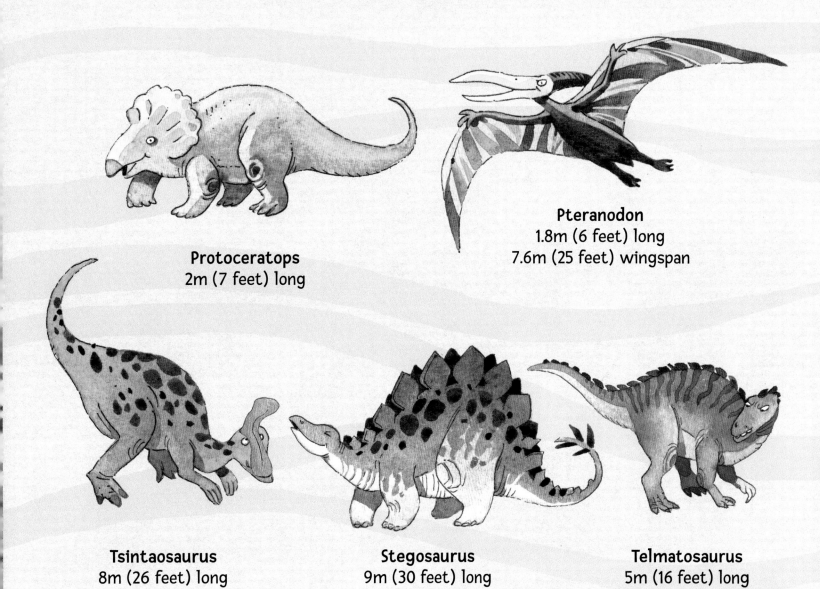

Protoceratops
2m (7 feet) long

Pteranodon
1.8m (6 feet) long
7.6m (25 feet) wingspan

Tsintaosaurus
8m (26 feet) long

Stegosaurus
9m (30 feet) long

Telmatosaurus
5m (16 feet) long

Supersaurus
35m (115 feet) long

Diplodocus
33.5m (110 feet) long – that's as long
as two buses parked end to end.

Up in the air

In the time of the dinosaurs, the skies were full of flying creatures called pterosaurs.

Quetzalcoatlus could stretch its wings 10m (33 feet) from end to end.

Tropeognathus had a wingspan of 8m (26 feet).

Zhejiangopterus had a very long beak compared to its body.

The largest pterosaur was called **hatzegopteryx**. Its HUGE wings were 12m (39 feet) from end to end. Each wing was taller than a double-decker bus.

Tupuxuara had an ENORMOUS crest on its head.

Rhamphorhynchus was only as big as a goose.

Anhanguera had long, spiky teeth.

Ornithocheirus was 3m (10 feet) tall when it walked on all fours.

Archaeopteryx was one of the world's first birds.

Big, scary monsters

The SCARIEST dinosaurs were towering monsters with big teeth and sharp claws.

Even the dinosaurs they hunted looked scary. They were covered in horns, spikes and rocky bumps to protect them.

Lift the pages and see how many of these dinosaurs you can find in the scene underneath.

Stenonychosaurus
2.5m (8 feet) long
May have eaten small
animals as well as plants

Bambiraptor
1.3m (4 feet) long
Ate other dinosaurs

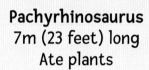

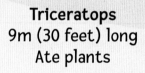

Pachyrhinosaurus
7m (23 feet) long
Ate plants

Triceratops
9m (30 feet) long
Ate plants

Therizinosaurus
10m (33 feet) long
May have eaten small
animals as well as plants

Tyrannosaurus
12.4m (40 feet) long
Ate other dinosaurs

Giganotosaurus
13m (43 feet) long
Ate other dinosaurs

Velociraptor
1.8m (6 feet) long
Ate other dinosaurs

Deinonychus
3.4m (11 feet) long
Ate other dinosaurs

Styracosaurus
5.5m (18 feet) long
Ate plants

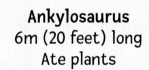

Pentaceratops
6m (20 feet) long
Ate plants

Sauropelta
6m (20 feet) long
Ate plants

Ankylosaurus
6m (20 feet) long
Ate plants

Carcharodontosaurus
12.5m (41 feet) long
Ate other dinosaurs

Spinosaurus
14m (46 feet) long
Ate other dinosaurs

Big, scary, meat-eating
dinosaurs are known as
theropods. Spinosaurus was
the longest known theropod.

Sea monsters

At the time of the dinosaurs, the seas were full of huge, fearsome creatures. Some were as big as whales, but with LONG necks, or MASSIVE, powerful jaws.

Liopleurodon had lots of very sharp teeth.

Fish-eating **mosasaurus** was a 13m (43 feet) monster.

Tylosaurus could leap out of the ocean to catch birds in the sky.

Thalassomedon was 11.6m (38 feet) long. Its LONG neck was half of its entire body.

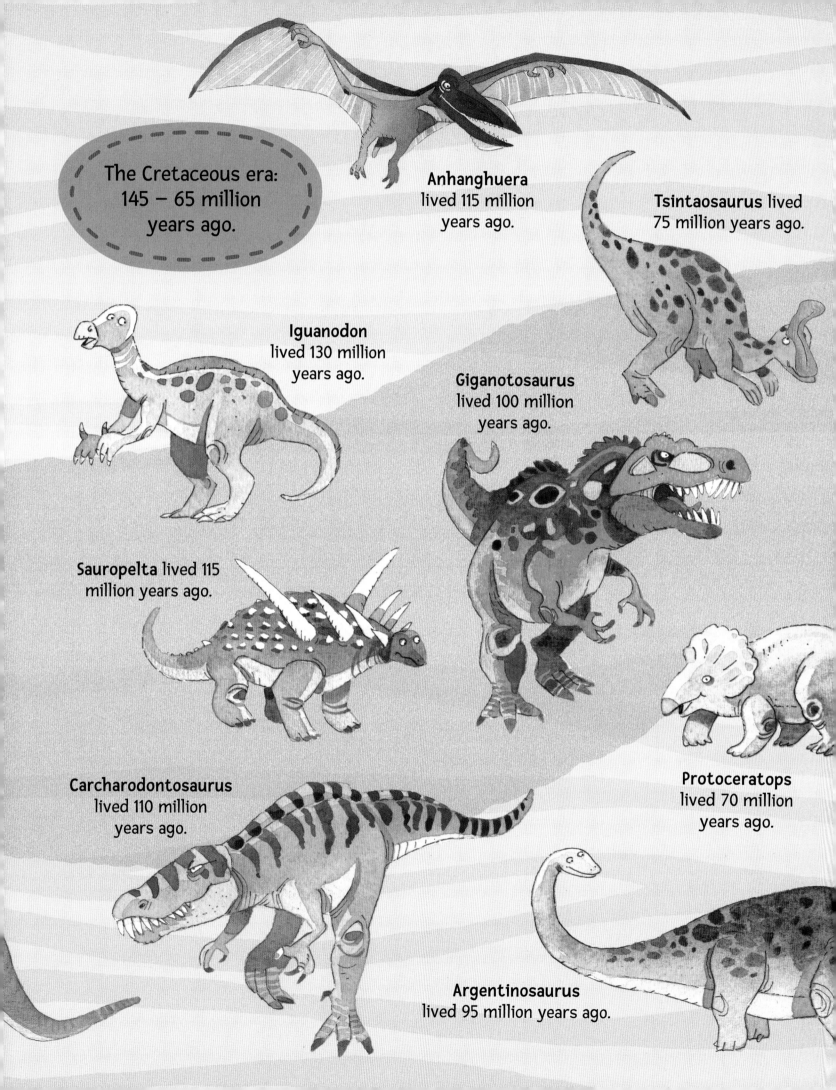

The Cretaceous era: 145 – 65 million years ago.

Anhanghuera lived 115 million years ago.

Tsintaosaurus lived 75 million years ago.

Iguanodon lived 130 million years ago.

Giganotosaurus lived 100 million years ago.

Sauropelta lived 115 million years ago.

Carcharodontosaurus lived 110 million years ago.

Protoceratops lived 70 million years ago.

Argentinosaurus lived 95 million years ago.

Stenonychosaurus lived 75 million years ago.

Brainiest dinosaur

Quetzalcoatlus lived 65 million years ago.

Dinosaur with the longest teeth (36cm / 14 inches)

Dinosaur with the longest horns (1m / 3 feet)

Tyrannosaurus lived 65 million years ago.

Triceratops lived 65 million years ago.

One of the fastest dinosaurs (65 km/h / 40 mph)

Ornithomimus lived 65 million years ago.

Elasmosaurus lived 65 million years ago.

The last dinosaurs died out 65 million years ago.

Heaviest dinosaur (100 tonnes / 110 tons)

Dinosaur footsteps

Some dinosaurs have left behind
footprints that you can still see today.

The footprints on these pages
are shown actual size.

A young
tyrannosaurus
footprint is 46cm
(18 inches) long.

An adult
tyrannosaurus
footprint is 83cm
(33 inches) long.

Usborne Quicklinks

For links to exciting websites about dinosaurs with videos, activities and a how to say guide to all the names in this book, scan the QR code or go to **usborne.com/Quicklinks** and type in the keywords "big dinosaurs."

Usborne Publishing is not responsible for the content of external websites. Children should be supervised online. Please follow the online safety guidelines at **usborne.com/Quicklinks**

Series designer: Mary Cartwright Series editor: Jane Chisholm
Additional design by Lisa Verrall and Laura Wood
Digital design by John Russell